WORKING STEAM
Stanier 8Fs

Jeff Ryan,
David McIntosh
and George Moon

Ian Allan
60th ANNIVERSARY

First published 2002

ISBN 0 7110 2894 X

© Ian Allan Publishing Ltd 2002

Published by Ian Allan Publishing

an imprint of Ian Allan Publishing Ltd, Hersham, Surrey KT12 4RG.
Printed by Ian Allan Printing Ltd, Hersham, Surrey KT12 4RG.

Code: 0210/B2

Title page: Late on the afternoon of Friday 19 June 1964, Saltley-based No 48339 (Horwich 1944) slowly eases her westbound Class 8 freight away from Blackwell and onto the infamous 1-in-37 Lickey Incline. The train will be slowly drawn forward, with a shunter pinning down sufficient wagon brakes to hold the train safely on the steep descent to Bromsgrove. The still-gaslit Blackwell station, seen in the background, finally lost its sparse service in 1966, the signalbox surviving until Gloucester power 'box took over in 1975. The footpath alongside the top of the Lickey Incline survives to this day, and still (if only rarely) occasionally echoes to the sound of a hard-working steam locomotive. *Ken Falconer*

Introduction

The Stanier '8F' locomotives were unique in two very different ways. Firstly they were the only locomotive design built by all the main works of the 'Big Four' (and three contractors as well), a total of 11 different works having been involved in the construction of a total of 852 locomotives of Britain's fourth-most numerous locomotive design. Secondly they were employed on regular work in no fewer than eight different countries — the UK, Italy, Turkey, Egypt, Palestine, Israel, Iraq and Persia (Iran). This wide range of operation by a single design of locomotive in both Europe and Asia is unequalled.

Sir William Stanier's seventh and most prolific design was built over a period of 11 years by three contractors — North British (158 locomotives), Vulcan Foundry (69) and Beyer Peacock (50) — and eight main-line company locomotive workshops — LMS Crewe (187 locomotives) and Horwich (75), SR Brighton (92), Eastleigh (23) and Ashford (15), LNER Darlington (53) and Doncaster (50) and finally the GWR at Swindon (80). Some confusion has been generated by the decision of the LNER to order 68 '8Fs' as Class O6, some 25 of which were built by the SR at Brighton and carried builder's plates declaring 'LNER built SR'! With the exception of Beyer Peacock, each builder is represented in the following pages. From 1940 to 1942 Beyer Peacock constructed 50 locomotives to a Ministry of Supply order, but the majority went overseas, with only a quarter eventually carrying a BR number.

The range of overseas operation of the '8Fs' saw 228 locomotives sent abroad, of which 23 were lost at sea. Significant allocations included Persia (originally 143 locomotives, reduced to 22 by 1946), then Palestine/Jordan (74), Egypt (62), Israel (24), Turkey (20), Italy (15) and Iraq (12). At the end of the war there were extensive reallocations within the Middle East. Many locomotives were moved on barges across the Euphrates and then mounted on narrow-gauge transporter wagons for the first stage of the journey between Basra and Baghdad, prior to making the long journey via Mosul, Aleppo, Beirut and Haifa before the final passage of the Sinai desert to Egypt.

From the point of view of the Motive Power Officer the '8Fs' were ideal heavy-freight power. Throughout the periods for which records are available the '8Fs' achieved consistent percentage availability figures in the mid-80s, average annual mileage of around 25,000 miles and at least 50,000 miles between general overhauls. To the Shedmaster, the '8Fs' were easily maintained, with piston and valve examinations progressively extended from 35,000 to 48,000 miles and then on an 'as reported' basis. Many locomotives went from one works repair to the next without having the cylinders opened up — a real achievement for a small-wheeled locomotive. In 1939 the LMS recorded not a single '8F' hot axlebox, compared to 1,235 generated by standard '4F' and '7F' locomotives. With footplate crews the '8Fs' were popular because they would steam on indifferent coal, were not over-sensitive to a variety of firing methods, and they could pull and run. The '8F' was an easy engine to prepare, although the lack of rocking-grates made disposal a much more onerous task. The preserved No 48773 has now been fitted with a drop-grate — a feature much appreciated by her largely volunteer crews. The less said about the temperamental exhaust steam injectors the better!

For the three authors — all directors of the Stanier 8F Locomotive Society — this book has been very much a labour of love. We have sought to obtain a reasonable geographical coverage of '8F'-hauled trains, our interpretation of the 'Working Steam' title excluding most shed scenes. The chosen selection reflects the predominance of the North West of England in '8F' deployment, particularly in the 1960s. Throughout this book we have used the 24-hour clock (adopted by BR in 1964) and the spelling of place names prevalent at the time of the particular photograph concerned. In June 1962 locomotive headcodes changed from an alphabetical to a numerical and, later, a four-character alpha-numeric system, and this too is reflected in the captions. Wherever possible, the photographer's notes have been used, in conjunction with relevant working timetables, in order to identify the actual trains pictured. Allocations quoted are those shown by the shedplate carried on the locomotive, or by contemporary documents.

We are truly grateful to the many photographers who responded so magnificently to our requests for assistance in the search for material. We have been overwhelmed by the quality and quantity of the images proffered — enough to compile two or even three volumes. We are also delighted that so many '8F'-hauled trains fortuitously appeared just before the arrival of the celebrity locomotive, which the photographer claimed to be actually waiting for!

In addition, special thanks are due to David Postle and his colleagues, for the superb facilities provided at the Kidderminster Railway Museum,

and also to Ron White of Colour-Rail. Derek Huntriss and Adrian White, meanwhile, proved excellent contacts for material, whilst Peter Groom has been invaluable in a number of ways. Directors of the Society, in particular Rob Newman, have also made a very helpful contribution, as have other friends of the Society who have responded freely with information.

Given the huge contribution made to freight operations by the 666 '8Fs' that operated in Great Britain, it is remarkable that no example was earmarked for the National Collection. The inspiration behind the decision to acquire No 8233/48773 is given in the text. For those who enjoy statistics it is a sobering thought that the locomotive has now been owned by the Society for 34 years — significantly longer than the 28 of her six previous owners.

Over the years the Society has expanded its activities. Members receive *Black Eight*, an excellent A4-size magazine covering a variety of topics. Access is available to the database of '8F' photographs, covering published material as well as that known to be in private collections. The website — www.8fsociety.co.uk — is increasingly popular. We are proud and honoured that, as a former Sapper herself, our locomotive is designated as an official memorial to military railwaymen of the Corps of Royal Engineers who fell in World War 2. During 2001 she became one of only a handful of standard-gauge locomotives to have achieved 100,000 miles in preservation, in the process contributing richly to the title of this album. Readers interested in receiving details of the Society are invited to contact our Membership Secretary at 73 Maesquarre Road, Betws, Ammanford, Carmarthenshire, SA18 2LF (tel: 01269 594865). This address may also be used as a contact point for any observations about the album and for contributions to the Society.

Finally, it is appropriate that we record our appreciation to our families, especially Rosemary, Katherine and Charlotte Ryan and Sandra Moon, for their patience and forbearance during the many hours of preparation of this album. We hope you enjoy the result.

Jeff Ryan, David McIntosh and George Moon
for and on behalf of The Stanier 8F Locomotive Society Ltd
July 2002

SCOTLAND

Polmadie-allocated No 48774 (NB 1940) makes a vigorous southbound climb up the 1-in-164 approach to Larbert with a Class 8 block load of Clackmannan coal on the ex-'Caley' main line from Stirling on Saturday 2 March 1963. The locomotive (formerly WD 320, LMS 8246, Persia, Egypt and then WD 501) is one of the three surplus WD locomotives acquired by BR from the Longmoor Military Railway in 1957. Allocated to Polmadie to meet a need for more heavy freight power to work the flow of imported iron ore from Glasgow's General Terminus quay to the new Ravenscraig steelworks, she was initially overhauled at Eastleigh. Originally intended to be given the number 90734, she was erroneously painted as 90743 before the decision was taken to allocate spare numbers at the end of the '8F' series. Polmadie's three '8Fs' were displaced by the new Clayton Type 1 diesels and put into store at the end of 1962, being reinstated after only a month, when the severe winter decimated their replacements. Withdrawn and stored again in July 1963, the three locomotives were again reinstated in November and put through Horwich Works before allocation to Kingmoor. *George Staddon*

Carrying Class E headlamps, Kingmoor's No 48536 (Doncaster 1945) accelerates her weedkiller special train up the 1-in-170 climb south from Alloway Junction, on the ex-GSW Ayr–Stranraer main line south of Ayr, in this view from May 1961. Alloway Junction was the junction for the branch to Girvan via Heads of Ayr, closed in 1968. The vanfits at the front of the train are used to carry the bagged weedkiller, and the tank wagons behind carry the water supply for the spray coach at the rear of the train. *Derek Cross*

On 1 July 1967 Nos 48380 (Horwich 1944) and 48115 (Crewe 1939) drag forward their heavy Class 5 block load of steel-making lime from Hardendale Quarry (Shap) to Ravenscraig northwards through Beattock station, prior to attaching the bankers for the 10-mile climb to Beattock Summit. The locomotives are allocated to Bolton and Heaton Mersey, on what one would expect to be Carnforth or Kingmoor work, so some borrowing of locomotives seems to have taken place. The train has a substantial fitted head of minfits to facilitate the maximum possible brake force (and load) when descending the long grades between Shap and Carlisle and between Beattock Summit and Carstairs. The deserted Beattock shed (66F), closed on 1 May 1967, is in the right background, and the up yard (behind the train) is busy with permanent-way trains ready for weekend re-laying activity. By this date the bankers will have been Clayton Type 1 diesels. Regular steam working into Scotland finished just over a month later, on 7 August 1967. *Ken Fairey*

THE NORTH WEST

Beneath a grey autumn sky in 1965, a footplateman going off duty gives a friendly wave to the crew in charge of Rose Grove (10F)-allocated No 48218 (NB 1942) as she slowly departs Kingmoor Yard on to the up goods line, towards Port Carlisle Junction and the Carlisle-avoiding line, with a special southbound train of empty vanfits. These are probably destined for Christmas parcels loading at one of the Lancashire parcels depots. Above the locomotive can be seen the turntable, shed and mechanical coaling plant of Kingmoor shed (12A). In the far distance are the lighting towers of the new Carlisle Kingmoor New Yard. Opened in 1963 at a cost of £4.5 million, at its peak it handled 134 trains and had the capacity to sort over 5,000 wagons daily over the hump into its 48 sorting sidings. With the decline in wagon-load freight, the hump was removed in 1981, with all sidings removed apart from a vestigial up fan remaining to handle all surviving traffic. *Vic Nutton/ Geoff Lumb collection*

Below: On Maundy Thursday (15 April) 1965 the bare countryside has been refreshed by a brief shower as the crew of an unidentified '8F' have spurned banking assistance from Tebay. With a typical 'white feather' at the safety valves, the locomotive makes light work of a sprint above Scout Green up the 1-in-75 towards Shap Summit with a lightweight 19-wagon Class 7 Bamfurlong (Wigan)–Carlisle mixed freight. In the background is the old A6, now displaced by the M6 which has so disfigured the present-day scene at this location. *Trevor Owen*

Right: On 6 August 1966 '8F' superpower approaches the stop at Tebay for banking assistance. Nos 48352 (Horwich 1944) and 48471 (Swindon 1945) roll through the Lune Gorge just north of Dillicar

troughs with a heavy train of prefabricated new concrete sleepered track panels being worked north ready for weekend re-laying work. The Class 8 headlamps indicate that the only brake power of the train, originating at Castleton PAD (pre-assembly depot), near Rochdale, is provided by the two locomotives and the brake van; Newton Heath shed has borrowed Royston's 48352 to assist its own 48471 to work this special out-of-gauge load of 'Salmon' wagons. The empty first wagon has been provided ready to accept the first panel of the lifted old track, which will then be removed from site by the same train, old panels simply replacing the new ones. Note that No 48471 retains the GWR-type vacuum ejector fitted from 1956 to Swindon-built '8Fs' allocated to the Western Region. *Gavin Morrison*

Right: On 22 July 1966 Agecroft-allocated No 48224 (NB 1942) is working a Lostock Hall diagram as she races south along the West Coast main line, passing over Brock troughs, just south of Garstang, with the heavily loaded 6P52 14.42 Heysham Harbour Junction–Preston (North Union) freight. After running only 21 miles from Heysham, the fireman obviously has no need to take water from the troughs. In a reminder that railways were in the forefront of containerisation, the train is formed almost entirely of BD containers, loaded on Conflats, which will have arrived on the BR cargo ferry from Belfast. There are also three empty tank wagons returning from the ICI fertilizer plant at Heysham Moss to Haverton Hill. In the background is the almost-deserted new Preston Bypass (M6); the only southbound vehicle visible is one of the distinctive Charrington's Beer lorries. *Bert Holland*

Left: On 29 January 1968 Northwich's No 48063 (Vulcan Foundry 1936) is only days away from her March withdrawal as she climbs past the fine array of semaphore signals at Preston No 5 'box. The train is the 7L00 11.15 Oakleigh–Corkickle No 1 block load of Covhops, conveying soda ash from ICI Northwich to Marchon Chemicals at Whitehaven. At Corkickle the Covhops will be cable-hauled up the Corkickle Brake inclined plane to the Marchon plant, located on the top of a hill overlooking Whitehaven. This train went over to Class 40 diesel haulage from 4 March 1968.
Ken Horan

Right: On 11 April 1968 Rose Grove-allocated No 48062 (Vulcan Foundry 1936) puts on a spectacular display of power and fury as she accelerates away from the West Coast main line at Preston No 5 signalbox on the down slow line towards Kirkham and Fleetwood. The train is a Class 8 Rose Grove–Burn Naze North (for ICI) load of coal with a fitted head of 21-ton minfits. In the background is the goods warehouse at Preston (Maudland) goods depot.
Les Nixon

Below: The fireman on Kingmoor-allocated No 48612 (Ashford 1943) takes a breather, a bout of firing having created a spectacular display of exhaust as his locomotive accelerates her southbound express freight past Farington Curve Junction, just south of Preston, in June 1966. *Mike Chapman/Colour-Rail BRM624*

Right: On Saturday 4 November 1967 autumn leaves cause major adhesion problems at Mallerstang Common, just north of Ais Gill, for Newton Heath-allocated No 48090 (Vulcan Foundry 1937) heading the 6F40 09.10 Long Meg sidings (Newbiggin)–Widnes (Tanhouse Lane) block load of anhydrite for the United Sulphuric Acid Co of Widnes. Although the continuous slipping has inevitably played havoc with the fire, the locomotive has steam to spare and the steam sanders are fully on as she fights for adhesion, having taken nearly 50 minutes to struggle the six miles at 1 in 100 from Kirkby Stephen. These long-standing trains were more regularly worked by BR '9F' 2-10-0 locomotives, and the appearance of an '8F' on the Long Meg hoppers as late as 1967 was relatively unusual. *Gavin Morrison*

Left: Bright autumn sunshine highlights Wild Boar Fell, towering behind Crewe South-based No 48436 (Swindon 1944) as she storms up the last few yards of 1-in-100 to Ais Gill on 18 October 1967. The locomotive carries Class 8 headlamps (but no shedplate) with a southbound extra train of empty vanfits from Carlisle to the South. Despite the 48-mile climb to Ais Gill, the locomotive appears to be well in charge, with a 'white feather' visible at the safety valves. The fireman appears to have given the locomotive a last round of firing before sitting down for a welcome rest on the long down grade to Settle Junction. *Neville Simms*

Right: After the long haul up the 'Long Drag' to Blea Moor, Lostock Hall-allocated No 48077 (Vulcan Foundry 1936) rattles north on the easier grades through Dent in October 1967 with the 5L03 23.20 Camden–Carlisle express freight. Amidst the vanfits of sundries which form the staple traffic for this train, the fifth, sixth and seventh wagons are Conflats carrying empty FM insulated containers returning north from London's Smithfield market for more southbound loads of Scottish beef. Note also on the hillside above the station the dilapidated snow fences built to prevent drifting snow being blown into and filling the cutting in which the station stands. The station car park is unusually busy with a variety of 1960s-vintage cars, possibly related to a special train hauled by *Clun Castle* expected over Shap later that afternoon. *Trevor Owen*

Covered with a dusting of snow, Whernside dominates the background as Bolton-allocated No 48469 (Swindon 1945) accelerates away down the 1-in-100 grade towards Ribblehead after a water stop at Blea Moor in April 1967. The train is an up Class 8 freight from Carlisle to the South. At 60 miles from Carlisle, Blea Moor was a necessary water stop for southbound fast freights if, for any reason, Garsdale troughs, seven miles further north, had failed to fill the tender of such a free-steaming and economical locomotive as an '8F'. *Paul Riley/Restoration & Archiving Trust*

At Kirkham & Wesham on 4 April 1968, Patricroft-allocated No 48491 (Horwich 1945) has just taken water in the yard as an unidentified '8F' storms past with the 8P21 10.52 Burnley Central–Burn Naze North (for ICI). This block load of coal is loaded entirely in 24½-ton mineral wagons, reflecting the larger tippler capacity at this industrial location. Note that there are four running lines still in use between Preston and Kirkham and that in the middle distance are the backs of the semaphore signals for the formerly three-way junction of the routes to Blackpool Central via Lytham (cut back to Blackpool South November 1964), Central direct via Marton (closed September 1966) and to Blackpool North/Fleetwood via Poulton. *Peter Fitton*

Almost at journey's end and within one month of the end of regular BR steam, Rose Grove's No 48340 (Horwich 1944) wheels the 8P19 12.00 Burnley Central–Wyre Dock power station coal train round the apex of the triangle at Poulton No 5 'box towards Fleetwood on 10 July 1968. The passenger service to Fleetwood had been cut back to Wyre Dock (renamed Fleetwood) station in 1966 and was closed finally in 1970. Note that this train is composed entirely of 16-ton mineral wagons, in contrast to the 8P21 at Kirkham in the previous photograph. *Peter Fitton*

On Friday 2 August 1968 Rose Grove-allocated No 48423 (Swindon 1943) gets into her stride beyond Bamber Bridge's tall outer home signal up the 1-in-99 climb of Houghton Bank, whilst working the very last BR regularly scheduled steam-hauled freight train, the 7N99 18.30 Preston (North Union)–Healey Mills. Under the control of Driver Dick Lord, No 48423 worked as far as Rose Grove, where both locomotive and crew were relieved, arriving back on shed at 22.10.

The town (now city) of Preston fills the background, while the overbridge behind the train carries the M6 Preston Bypass. As the safety valves begin to lift, the fireman (wearing typical North West knotted-handkerchief headgear) appears to have just put on the live steam injector to keep this apparently free-steaming locomotive quiet. The second, to fifth wagons on the train are empty plate wagons returning to Scunthorpe. *Roy Hobbs*

Below: The driver of Rose Grove-allocated No 48668 (Brighton 1944) watches patiently for the road to clear on a bright but frosty 7 December 1965, whilst his locomotive quietly simmers at the west end of Blackburn station with a coal train. Gaslights flicker on the platform and the signalman's coal stove smokes gently, but the fire-devils intended to keep the parachute water tank from freezing appear to have gone out. *Bert Holland*

Right: On Saturday 18 May 1968, just west of Rose Grove, locally allocated No 48062 (Vulcan Foundry 1936) assists a Skipton Standard Class 4 4-6-0 with a double load of new ballast being staged forward ready for weekend engineering works. The train had originated at Swinden Quarry on the Grassington branch and will have come from Skipton via Colne on a line destined to survive only until February 1970. Behind the train can be seen the town of Burnley and the mechanical coaling plant at Rose Grove shed, which would close just over two months later. *Derek Penney*

Left: On Saturday 18 May 1968 a group of lineside enthusiasts stand in awe as No 48410 (Swindon 1943), banked by No 48519 (Doncaster 1944), both allocated to Rose Grove, storm the last few yards up the grade to Copy Pit with another load of westbound Yorkshire coal. The crew are obviously enjoying playing to the gallery, both locomotives having 'white feathers' at the safety valves, indicating locomotives (despite being at the end of their working lives) still in total command of the work for which they were designed more than 30 years before. The linesiders were awaiting a special passenger train hauled by *Flying Scotsman,* and were no doubt delighted with this unexpected display of brute '8F' power.
Trevor Owen

Right: It is 27 February 1968 and the windows in Copy Pit signalbox are rattling with the sound and fury of Rose Grove-allocated No 48062 (Vulcan Foundry 1936) as she breasts the summit with an eastbound train of empty 16-ton mineral wagons returning to Yorkshire for further loads. The redundant signal arm on the bracket signal gave access to the former bank-engine turn-back siding, removed in anticipation of the end of banking some five months hence. *Neville Simms*

Below: The now-preserved No 48773 (NB 1940), formerly WD 307, LMS 8233, ISR 41.109, WD70307 and WD500, is nicely framed by the setting sun at 21.30 in this June 1968 shot of a Rose Grove–Moston load of coal, coasting downgrade from Sough Tunnel across Entwistle Viaduct between Blackburn and Bolton. The locomotive was based at Bolton (9K) from 21 September 1964 until closure of the depot on 29 June 1968, her final five weeks in BR service being spent at Rose Grove (10F). As the '8F' in the best overall condition, No 48773 was selected for preservation by the Stanier 8F Locomotive Society and since 1969 has been based on the Severn Valley Railway. *Frank Cronin*

Right: The present headquarters of the East Lancs Railway, Bury Bolton Street looks a little different at lunchtime on 7 July 1965. Newton Heath-allocated No 48321 (Crewe 1944) is hauling the Colne–Red Bank empty newspaper vans, running late and diverted from their usual route via Blackburn and Bolton. Alongside, Bolton-based Stanier 2-6-4T No 42626 is engaged in station-pilot duties, whilst both the right- and left-hand platforms are occupied by Manchester–Bury electric units. Note the unique side-contact 1,200V DC third rail visible between the steam locomotives. The Manchester–Bury electrics were withdrawn in 1991 when the line was diverted to the new Bury Interchange station and converted to the 750V DC overhead Metrolink light-rail system. *Bert Holland*

Left: Bolton-allocated No 48773 (NB 1940) has just arrived at the paper mills of Yates, Duxbury & Son Ltd, Heap Bridge (near Heywood), in the summer of 1967. The locomotive is working the afternoon 'Target 53' trip from Bury, the wagons containing china clay and coal having being tripped from Brewery sidings, Miles Platting, by the same locomotive earlier in the day. The Peckett *May* (Works No 1370, built 1915) was the youngest of the three works shunting engines. The yellow cabside stripe has been applied to No 48773 because the WD clack valves fitted to the boilers on Nos 48773-5 infringed the 13ft 1in height restriction, most other '8Fs' being only 12ft 10in high. The stripe was to ban restricted locomotives from working under the 25kV overhead line equipment south of Crewe, where tighter clearances had been adopted. However, as No 48773 had lost her WD clack-fitted boiler during a visit to Crewe Works in June 1966, the yellow stripe was not applicable and had obviously been applied in error ! *Frank Cronin*

Left: Running under clear signals, Bolton-allocated No 48380 (Horwich 1944) clatters through a snowy Rochdale with the 7N67 12.57 Middleton Junction–Carlton coal empties from Chadderton power station on Wednesday 6 February 1968. On the right, two permanent-way staff (with not a high-visibility vest in sight) trudge through the snow to Rochdale West 'box, with brushes at the ready for point-clearing duties. *Richard S. Greenwood*

On a bright and sunny 7 July 1965 Mold Junction-allocated No 48090 (Vulcan Foundry 1937) arrives at Hartshead CEGB Staley & Millbrook sidings with a train of Point of Ayr coal from Mold Junction. Staley & Millbrook was located just east of Stalybridge on the Micklehurst loop line between Stalybridge and Diggle, on the opposite side of the valley from the existing Diggle line. The Micklehurst loop closed to passengers in September 1964 and to all traffic in October 1966 between Diggle and Staley & Millbrook, meaning that coal from the east had henceforward to reverse at Stalybridge until Hartshead power station closed in the 1990s. The photo was taken during an LCGB visit to see the power station's fireless shunting locomotive *Hartshead. Bert Holland*

Left: In January 1968 Bolton-allocated No 48425 (Swindon 1943) stands on the up through line at Manchester Victoria with a block load of coal. The guard is lifting the wagon handbrakes, which he has pinned down just over a mile away at Miles Platting before the descent of the 1-in-47/59 grade. With no more brake force available to control the train than that supplied by the brakes on the locomotive and the guard's handbrake in his van, the train could safely descend any appreciable gradient only by the application of a carefully judged number of wagon handbrakes. The guard would carefully pin down sufficient wagon brakes as the train slowly moved on to the downgrade until the driver indicated, by the requisite whistle code, that he felt sufficient brake force had been applied. A steady descent would then be followed, as in this picture, by a stop at the bottom of the grade to uplift wagon handbrakes before proceeding — a slow and tedious process. The photographer is standing on the famous Platform 11, for many years Britain's longest platform (at 2,194ft), which linked Victoria and Exchange stations. *Vic Nutton/Geoff Lumb collection*

Left: On 1 June 1968 Newton Heath's No 48369 (Horwich 1944), running tender-first, waits for the road at Deal Street signalbox, at the western end of Manchester Exchange station. The train is a transfer of 'cripples' (defective wagons) for grading at Brindle Heath sidings, Agecroft, prior to repair at Horwich Works. The distinctive building in the background is Threlfalls Brewery, which for many years contributed a distinctive aroma to this part of Salford. *Keith Preston*

On 17 April 1968 Heaton Mersey-allocated No 48765 (Doncaster 1946) coasts past Woodley Junction towards Stockport Tiviot Dale with a Class 8 Tinsley–Warrington train of house coal. The '8F' will have collected her train at Godley Junction, replacing a Class EM1 (later Class 76) DC electric locomotive which will have hauled the train over the Woodhead line from Sheffield. In the station yard the local scrap merchant is busy loading wagons with scrap iron for the furnaces of Sheffield, whilst the coal merchant's lorry is ready to depart with another delivery of house coal loaded in 1cwt sacks. Note the typical MS&L signalbox in the background. This line closed as a through route to Cheadle Junction in 1980, being retained as a long siding for access to a roadstone depot at Portwood and the Greater Manchester Waste Transfer station at Bredbury. No 48765 was built as LNER 'O6' class No 3160, being renumbered 3560 in 1947 and transferred to the LMS in October 1947. *Bill Potter/Kidderminster Railway Museum*

On 30 March 1968 locally allocated No 48252 (NB 1941) heads tender-first away from Heaton Mersey sidings and across the River Mersey with a long Class 8 train of empty 16-ton minerals for Godley Junction and the Woodhead route to Sheffield. The fireman has plenty of steam available, ready for the climb through Stockport Tiviot Dale station to Woodley Junction. The photograph was taken from the embankment of the former Midland Railway direct line from Cheadle Heath to Manchester Central, closed in 1969. The entire scene is now devoid of railways and is dominated by the M60 Manchester orbital motorway. *Les Nixon*

In this June 1939 shot, hand-tinted by the photographer, LMS No 8089 (Vulcan Foundry 1937) of Heaton Mersey shed (19D) is pictured heading 16 ICI limestone hoppers through Cheadle CLC station. The headlamp code is an LMS Manchester-area routeing code. The 84 'Hoppers' (a fleet ultimately expanded to 152 wagons) entered service in December 1938 and faithfully carried up to 3 million tons of limestone from Tunstead Quarry to the three ICI plants at Northwich for 59 years, until 30 December 1997. No 8089 was one of the initial five '8Fs' allocated to Heaton Mersey for this service. The Heaton Mersey locomotives were initially outbased at the LNER Northwich depot for these trains which, from 1949, were worked by Northwich-based locomotives. There were up to seven trains a day for seven days a week for 364 days a year until 1979, when the last operation on Boxing Day took place. '8F' power reigned supreme on the 'Hoppers' for 25 years, from 1938 to 1963, not being totally displaced until 1968. No 8089 had been requisitioned by the War Department in 1941 for service in Persia. It was one of eight, loaded at Swansea in the hold of the steamer *Pentridge Hall*, which suffered so much damage in a severe storm off Land's End that they had to be returned to North British at Glasgow for repairs. Four other '8Fs', loaded as deck cargo, were forever lost overboard in the same storm. After repairs and by now no longer required in Persia, No 8089 went on loan to the LMS in 1942. It was the stirring performances of the '8Fs' on the 'Hoppers' that inspired the formation of the Stanier 8F Locomotive Society and the preservation of LMS No 8233 (BR No 48773). *Bill Potter/Kidderminster Railway Museum*

Approaching Acton Grange Junction on 28 May 1966, the fireman looks back towards the rear of his train from Edge Hill-allocated No 48249 (NB 1940) as she crawls past spilt soda ash and debris at Moore. Here, two weeks earlier, a collision had taken place between a Class 40-hauled sleeping-car train and the runaway detached rear portion of an '8F'-hauled Northwich–St Helens train of Covhops. The train is a Class 8 through freight from Severn Tunnel Junction and is approaching its destination at Warrington Walton Old Junction yard. Notice to the left of the line the earthworks for the original formation of the main line, abandoned in the 1890s when construction of the Manchester Ship Canal required a new and higher alignment.
Hugh Ballantyne

With the Royal Liver Building prominent in the background on the other side of the River Mersey, Stoke-allocated No 48085 (Vulcan Foundry 1937) prepares to depart from Morpeth Dockyard in Birkenhead on Sunday 16 April 1967 with the 4K25 18.40 Irish cattle special to Chester and Crewe. Some of the cattle wagons will be worked forward from Chester on a Holyhead–York train to Ordsall Lane for the Manchester City abattoir at Philips Park or on a Holyhead–Banbury cattle special. The Class 03 diesel shunter on the left had brought the loaded cattle wagons up over the MD&HB lines from the lairage behind Woodside Landing Stage, where the cattle had been rested after their Irish Sea crossing, courtesy of B&I Line. Under a very long-standing arrangement, BR and its predecessors provided the shunting locomotives for all the dock lines at Birkenhead. Another sign of the Irish Sea shipping traffic at Morpeth Dock is the Conflat A wagon, in the middle of the picture, loaded with a light-blue-painted insulated FM meat container. *Edgar Richards*

Left: The young fireman of Crewe South-allocated No 48255 (NB 1941) gives the photographer a friendly smile as they roll the 5K10 19.15 Morpeth Dock–Crewe (Basford Hall) express freight on the up fast line through Hooton on 20 August 1966. The long train conveys traffic from Birkenhead Docks, from Shore Road goods depot and from the Lever Bros chemical complex at Port Sunlight. Traffic requirements justified four running lines north of Ledsham Junction on this ex-LNW/GW 'Birkenhead Joint' line. *Hugh Ballantyne*

Below: A very grimy Mold Junction-allocated No 48259 (NB 1941) is only a short distance from home as she crosses the River Dee bridge on the down fast line between Crane Street and Saltney Junction with a Class H freight in this August 1959 view. Behind the train can be seen the skyline of the city of Chester and its unique circular Roodee racecourse. The very mixed load of the train suggests that the day's repairs from Chester wagon shops have been picked up at Chester for onwards transit from Mold Junction yard. This view is largely unchanged today, except that only the two former slow lines survive. *Geoff Hunt/Colour-Rail BRM1767*

Left: At least five '8Fs' feature in this view of the turntable and coaling stage at Northwich (8E) shed on the evening of Saturday 18 May 1963. In the foreground, Kirkby-allocated No 48643 (Brighton 1943) has been turned and serviced ready for a return with coal empties to her Nottinghamshire home, whilst locally allocated No 48155 (Crewe 1942) rolls another load of coal empties into the up yard past typical CLC lower-quadrant signals. Two further '8Fs' sit on the coal road, whilst a fellow class member drops down towards the turntable amidst the typical steam-shed scene of piles of ash and clinker deposited from countless previous locomotive disposals. *Richard S. Greenwood*

THE PEAK DISTRICT

Right: Crewe South-allocated No 48729 (Brighton 1944) is nicely framed by Edale's starter signal in this 1967 picture. The train is climbing the 1-in-100 westbound grade along the Hope Valley line towards Cowburn Tunnel with a Grindleford–Heaton Mersey Class 8 special load of sheeted 16-ton minerals conveying fluorspar. In the background is the 1,936ft-high shoulder of Kinder Scout, the first hurdle for walkers on the Pennine Way, which begins here at Edale. When built at Brighton, No 48729 was the last of an order from the LNER for 25 Class O6 locomotives and was originally numbered 7675, being renumbered 3124 and then 3524 in 1947 before being sent on loan to the LMS in exchange for surplus WD 2-8-0s. *Les Nixon*

Left: On 12 September 1960 Bescot-allocated No 48602 (Eastleigh 1943), running with an ex-'Jubilee' Fowler tender, gets into her stride up the 1-in-269/177 climb on the up slow line between Basford Hall and Betley Road, south of Crewe, with a southbound Class H freight. Despite the rather grimy appearance, No 48602 appears to be in fine form, with only a slightly discoloured exhaust, 'white feather' at the safety valves and injector humming. Notice the well-used telegraph poles and wires required on both sides of this busy stretch of the West Coast main line — a feature long gone from the modern railway scene. *Derek Cross*

Left: The fireman on Stourton's No 48274 (NB 1942) keeps a wary eye on the photographer as his locomotive storms away up the 1-in-89 gradient on the up fast line south from New Mills South Junction. The train is a Class 7 load of empty iron-ore tipplers, probably returning from Glazebrook steelworks to the East Midlands ironstone mines, in this wintry view from the mid-'60s. To the right of the locomotive, located between the fast and slow lines, is Gowhole marshalling yard, responsible, jointly with Rowsley, for marshalling freight traffic over the Midland main line via Peak Forest, which closed as a through route in 1967. *Vic Nutton/Geoff Lumb collection*

Right: On 3 February 1968 Buxton's No 48327 (Crewe 1944) makes a spectacular display of exhaust as she climbs the up slow line's 1-in-90 gradient between Buxworth and Chinley station with a Gowhole–Peak Forest Class 8 freight. In 1902 this section of former Midland Railway route was widened to four tracks, including the opening-out of Buxworth Tunnel to form a deep cutting. Today's higher speeds and the reduced demands of modern traffic levels have allowed a return to the original two tracks, with the former fast lines (nearer the camera) now carrying all traffic. *Derek Huntriss*

Left: At Chinley North Junction on 18 November 1967 Buxton's No 48744 (Darlington 1946) sets a truly volcanic scene as she storms across the junction with a Class 8 trip of empty limestone hoppers and 16-ton minerals from Gowhole to Peak Forest. *Neville Simms*

Right: The snow-white exhaust of Buxton's No 48442 (Swindon 1944) is picked out by a bright winter sun in this 3 February 1968 snowy shot between Chinley South and Chapel-en-le-Frith Central. The extreme right- and left-hand tracks are goods loops, and, owing to engineering work in Dove Holes Tunnel, single-line working was in operation over the down line between Chinley South and Peak Forest. The Class 8 trip from Gowhole to Peak Forest will shortly back across onto the down line before proceeding south. The previous night had seen frantic activity at Buxton shed as members of the MNA enthusiast group returned No 48442 to pristine condition. Attempts to photograph the outward trip from Buxton to Gowhole were thwarted by early-morning fog. *Derek Huntriss*

Left: On 22 April 1967 Heaton Mersey-allocated No 48723 (Brighton 1944) rolls downgrade out of Dove Holes Tunnel towards Chinley with the Saturdays-only 8F56 12.00 Tunstead–Runcorn (Folly Lane) block load of Covhops, loaded with lime. Note how the telegraph wires stride above the tunnel and over the hillside and the ventilation shaft on the hill top. No 48723 was built by the SR at Brighton as LNER No 7669 to an order from the latter for 68 Class O6 2-8-0s. *Neville Simms*

Right: The evidence of enthusiasts' cleaning work is apparent as Buxton-allocated No 48465 (Swindon 1945) slowly draws her Buxton-bound train of loaded 21-ton coal hoppers out of the sidings at Peak Forest on 21 October 1967. The locomotive had arrived double-heading with No 48191 on a train from Gowhole. The unusual white vehicle in the siding on the right was provided to remove casualties from the quarry in locations inaccessible to an ambulance. Buxton's '8F' duties were confined mainly to serving the needs of the area's numerous local quarries and lime works. Whichever route they took, hard climbing was the order of the day, from the cavernous excavations at Tunstead to the slippery 1-in-90 climb through Dove Holes Tunnel. *Derek Huntriss*

Below: There is fresh snow on the ground on 17 February 1968 as Heaton Mersey-allocated No 48365 (Horwich 1944) storms the 1-in-90 grade past a fine wooden ex-Midland Railway bracket signal at Great Rocks Junction with the 8F56 Tunstead–Runcorn 'covhops'. Above the locomotive can be seen the exhaust of the '8F' banker, which will assist the train from Tunstead into the loop at Peak Forest. The milepost records 163 miles from St Pancras via Derby and Matlock and into the Peak District, which route had closed the previous year. On the right, the diesel shunting locomotive in the sidings, attached to some brake vans, is an ICI-owned English Electric 0-6-0, identical in most respects to the BR Class 08. *Les Nixon*

Right: Less than a week before the end of local steam operations, Patricroft-allocated No 48775, (Crewe 1937 as LMS 8025, WD 583, Persia, Egypt and then WD 512), threads through Ashwood Dale on the approach to Buxton (Midland) with a Gowhole–Buxton trip on 28 February 1968. Steam working in the area ceased from 4 March 1968 with the closure of Northwich (8E), Trafford Park (9E) and Buxton (9L) sheds. One of the three ex-WD locomotives bought by BR in 1957, No 48775 retains her WD clacks but has escaped the 'yellow stripe' which should therefore have been applied. This locomotive survived to the end of steam, being withdrawn finally from Lostock Hall in August 1968. *Peter Fitton*

YORKSHIRE

Below: The end was less than three months away as No 48410 (Swindon 1943) negotiates the sharp curve off the Calder Valley main line at Hall Royd Junction, Todmorden, with a loaded coal train from the Yorkshire coalfields to Rose Grove on Saturday 18 May 1968. No 48519 (Doncaster 1944) waits in the background to act as banker up the steep climb, mainly at 1 in 65, to Copy Pit Summit. Both locomotives are based at Rose Grove. On page 22 the same train is shown later in its journey. *Gavin Morrison*

Right: Long-term Holbeck resident No 48067 (Vulcan Foundry 1936) leaves Whitehall Junction at Leeds with a 15-coach St Pancras–Glasgow St Enoch empty stock train on Thursday 7 September 1961. The stock was being used for the 'Starlight Special' reduced-fare overnight Anglo-Scottish services. Above the second coach, 'Britannia' No 70053 *Moray Firth* waits to follow with 17 empty coaches for similar duties. Meanwhile, visible above the '8F', 'Jubilee' No 45606 *Falkland Islands* turns on the Holbeck triangle prior to returning home to Carnforth with the 13.54 Leeds City–Carnforth passenger train. *Gavin Morrison*

On 19 August 1967 Royston-allocated No 48222 (NB 1942) is in easy command on the gently rising grade with a 1,200-ton, 50-wagon westbound load of Yorkshire coal past the deserted shed at Mirfield (56D), closed in January 1967. Alongside the shed can be seen the distinctive American-style 'speed signals' installed at Mirfield by the LMS in 1932 in an attempt to keep the heavy-freight traffic moving smoothly on this busy trans-Pennine route. The 'Green over Red' of the down slow-line signal is a 'clear' aspect. This installation, unique in the UK, survived until Healey Mills power 'box took over control in 1969. *Gerald T. Robinson*

Left: On 18 October 1967 No 48168 (Crewe 1943) of Heaton Mersey passes Longwood Goods on the up slow line, nearly two miles west of Huddersfield, as she gets into her stride against the six-mile climb at 1 in 105 to Standedge Tunnel. The train is the 20-wagon Leeds Neville Hill–Stanlow empty tanks, by this date more usually hauled by a Birkenhead Standard '9F' 2-10-0. At this time there were still four running lines open between Huddersfield and Marsden. *Gavin Morrison*

Below left: Stourton-allocated No 48311 (Crewe 1943) has had a Bank Holiday outing to the seaside as she roars past Driffield with a return excursion from Bridlington to the West Riding just after 6pm on Whit Monday (22 May) 1961. This unusual working was followed a few minutes later by another Stourton '8F', No 48703, working a 10-coach return excursion, presumably to Leeds. Both trains would have followed the direct line from Driffield to Selby via Market Weighton, which did not close until June 1965. *Don Rowland*

THE EAST MIDLANDS

In August 1964 Crewe South-allocated No 48729 (Brighton 1944 as LNER 'O6' No 7675) approaches Bagworth Junction with a Colwick–Crewe Class 8 freight, loaded principally with gypsum from East Leake in sheeted 16-ton minerals. The train will take the ex-GNR line over Bennerley Viaduct to Derby Friargate and Egginton Junction to reach the ex-North Staffs Derby–Stoke line. In the background are New Basford carriage sidings, which served Nottingham Victoria station — less than two miles south through Sherwood Rise and Mansfield Road tunnels. The north approach cutting to the former can be seen behind the train, in the far distance beyond the typical GC island platform structure of New Basford station. *Don Beecroft/ Colour-Rail BRE664*

On Wednesday 31 August 1966 — only five days before closure of the GC as a through route — Westhouses based No 48393 (Horwich 1945) emerges from Mansfield Road Tunnel and passes Nottingham Victoria North signalbox with a Class 7 unfitted freight. The train is composed almost entirely of empty iron-ore tipplers returning from Stanton Gate to the Vale of Belvoir ironstone mines reached by way of the Nottingham–Grantham line. Before the closure in 1960 of the direct line from Leen Valley Junction to Colwick via Daybrook, caused by mining subsidence to a tunnel, this train would not have needed to pass through Nottingham Victoria station. The station finally closed on 4 September 1967 and has been replaced by the Victoria Shopping Centre. Today nothing remains except for the clock tower and bricked-up tunnel portal tucked away at the back of the car park.
Peter Fitton/Colour-Rail BRE1290

Leicester-allocated No 48149 (Crewe 1942) waits for the road south at Wigston South Junction sidings on 22 August 1959. The train appears largely to be conveying empty wooden pallets (for brick traffic) loaded into wagons, more of which can be seen in the immediate left foreground. The branch to the left leads, via Wigston Glen Parva Junction, to Nuneaton and Birmingham. Note the smart terrace of railway cottages behind the locomotive. *Michael Mensing*

Right: With at least 75 empty coal wagons in tow, Nottingham-based No 48117 (Crewe 1939) approaches Glendon South Junction, north of Kettering, on 30 May 1959. Judging by the amount of coal in her tender, the '8F' cannot have taken over this Cricklewood (Brent)–Toton train south of Wellingborough. The train is on the down slow line, heading for the usual and more easily graded route north via Corby, Melton Mowbray and the Syston North curve. *Trevor Owen*

Left: Cricklewood-based No 48538 (Doncaster 1945) coasts along the up slow line past Finedon Road signalbox at Wellingborough with a southbound Class E express freight on 16 July 1959. Stationary on the down slow line is one of the 10 locally based Franco-Crosti '9F' 2-10-0s, waiting to drop onto Wellingborough shed. Above the train, a tender-first Derby '4F' 0-6-0 is drawing a long loaded coal train out of the busy Wellingborough yard, which fills the background scene. The yard staff's bicycle shed appears to contain a typical 1950s collection of bicycles, a moped and a Lambretta scooter. The sidings to the left led to Wellingborough Furnaces, where local ore was smelted to pig iron. *Ken Fairey*

Below: Woodford Halse-based No 48027 (Vulcan Foundry 1936) departs southwards towards Culworth Junction from her home station on the morning of Saturday 18 April 1964. The long Class 8 freight is conveying a very mixed load of vans, pipes, steel and a tank wagon in the fitted head, with two separate blocks of house coal trailing behind. The train is probably heading for Neasden, with a planned detachment at Aylesbury. The branch leading off to the left is the chord to the ex-Stratford-upon-Avon & Midland Junction line to Fenny Compton, Stratford and Broom Junction. Above the rear of the train, an ex-GW tender locomotive is arriving with a northbound transfer of empty coal wagons from Banbury. Nothing now remains of the railway at Woodford Halse. *Neville Simms*

Left: Running under the newly erected overhead lines, locally based No 48453 (Swindon 1944) rounds Queensville curve at Stafford with a local trip from Lea Hall colliery at Rugeley on 6 October 1962. *Michael Mensing*

Below: On 22 February 1960 Bescot's recently ex-works No 48762 (Doncaster 1946 as LNER 'O6' No 3157), complete with Fowler tender, hauls a failed Gloucester DMU set through Great Barr on its way back to its base at Ryecroft, Walsall. The former steam shed at Ryecroft had been closed in June 1958 in order to create the West Midlands' first DMU depot, its steam allocation having been transferred to Bescot. *Eric Russell/Colour-Rail BRM1715*

Left: In the late afternoon of 2 October 1959, Wellingborough-allocated No 48381 (Horwich 1944) trundles a long mixed Toton–Washwood Heath Class H freight along the Derby–Birmingham main line, just east of Water Orton. The cooling towers in the background are those of Hams Hall 'A', 'B' and 'C' power stations, now the site of a rail-served distribution park.
Michael Mensing

Left: Outside her home depot of Saltley on Saturday 28 July 1962, No 48101 (Crewe 1939) draws forward past Duddeston Road signalbox ready to be banked up the Camp Hill line towards King's Norton with a Class 5 fast fitted freight from Washwood Heath to the West. The Camp Hill line passed alongside the Birmingham City football ground at St Andrews, and the passage of a slowly moving steam-hauled freight train, plus the banker, could sometimes create visibility problems on the pitch. On the left is the Saltley Gas Works, now the site of Saltley power 'box and the new West Coast Main Line Control Centre. *Trevor Owen*

Above: Gloucester-allocated No 48172 (Crewe 1943) has arrived at the south end of the LNW side of the old Birmingham New Street station at lunchtime on Friday 12 April 1963 with a Class 3 parcels from Gloucester and Worcester. The star on the cabside indicates a locomotive with 50% reciprocating balance and therefore suitable for 50mph timed fast-freight (and parcels) trains. Despite the date, it has yet to be fitted with the BR Automatic Warning System, with which most locomotives were fitted from 1960. *Neville Simms*

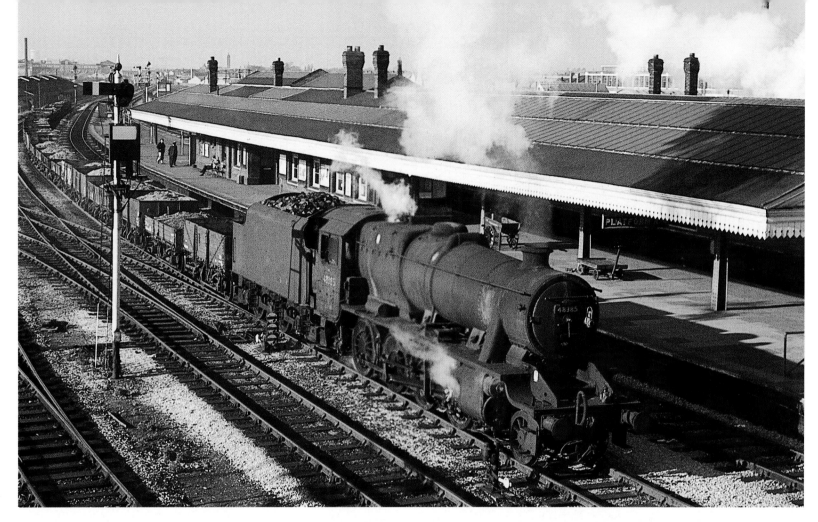

Left: Shrewsbury-allocated No 48724 (Brighton 1944, as LNER 'O6' No 7670) slowly draws a Class J local freight on the up through line into the north end of Birmingham Snow Hill station in the spring of 1962. The train is probably a transfer from Winson Green or Hockley freight depots to the marshalling yard at Bordesley. On the far right a GW 'Hall' engaged on station-pilot duties sits on empty stock. *John Edgington*

Above: A typically work-stained Saltley '8F', No 48385 (Horwich 1945), starts a full load of engineers' spoil, loaded after a re-ballasting deep dig, along the up goods line at Tyseley on Saturday 6 November 1965. The train is probably heading for the engineer's tip at Honeybourne, west of Stratford-upon-Avon. On the left is Tyseley carriage shed, at this date still serving Snow Hill and Moor Street stations. *Michael Mensing*

Left: Deep in former GW territory, late in the afternoon of 17 March 1962, Rugby-allocated No 48559 (Darlington 1945) makes easy work of the 1-in-110 climb up the down goods line on Hatton Bank, north of Leamington. The Class E express freight is a block load of Bedfordshire bricks, conveyed entirely in fitted high goods (FHG) wagons. This regular through-working was worked by a Rugby locomotive, often a 'Super D', via the Rugby–Leamington line (closed 1966) as far as Hatton. Again, the 'white feather' at the safety valves shows a locomotive in complete mastery of the task. *Derek Penney*

Above right: On 23 April 1966 Burton-allocated No 48056 (Vulcan Foundry 1936) heads for home from Nuneaton, crossing the A444 with a Banbury–Burton block load of coal empties. The train has left Weddington Junction and is heading for Shackerstone, Overseal and Moira West over what is now in part the preserved 'Battlefield Line'. The period roadsigns and the empty A-road add some 1960s atmosphere to this typical steam-era shot. This line closed to passengers as early as 1931 and finally to freight in 1969. *Trevor Owen*

Right: Willesden-allocated No 48601 (Eastleigh 1943), attached to a Fowler tender and running under clear signals, coasts past Ashby Junction, Nuneaton, on the up fast line with a long Class C express freight on Saturday 11 March 1961. The branch line curving away to the right behind the train leads via Weddington Junction to Shackerstone, Moira West and Burton. The overbridge crossing the main line in the distance is the chord line linking Weddington Junction with Abbey Street Junction and the ex-MR line to Birmingham via Whitacre. *Michael Mensing*

Coalville-based No 48053 (Vulcan Foundry 1936) rolls an eastbound train of 30 empty 16-ton mineral wagons onto the Nuneaton-avoiding line at Abbey Street Junction on 3 October 1964. Judkins Quarry fills the background, while, just above the locomotive, the chord line descending to the Trent Valley line has by now acquired 25kV overhead line equipment; note the locomotive carries electrification warning flashes. The avoiding line between Abbey Street Junction and Midland Junction closed in May 1981, supposedly because of the condition of the bridge spanning the West Coast main line at the north end of Nuneaton (Trent Valley) station. It is now set to be reopened, as part of the West Coast main line's renewal project. Note in the immediate left foreground the assorted grades of house coal in the row of mineral wagons being unloaded in the coal merchant's siding. *Michael Mensing*

THE SOUTH EAST

Right: On the bright but frosty morning of Christmas Eve 1962, Bletchley-allocated No 48729 (Brighton 1944 as LNER 'O6' No 7675) arrives with the daily trip from Bletchley, at Park Street level crossing, Aylesbury, on the ex-LNWR Cheddington–Aylesbury High Street branch. The guard is about to open the level-crossing gates before shunting High Street goods yard. The branch lost its passenger service in February 1953 and finally closed to freight in December 1963.
Tommy Tomalin/Colour-Rail BRM1372

Below right: Recently ex works, Rugby-allocated No 48018 (Crewe 1937) approaches Tring on the down slow line under the newly energised overhead catenary with the Class 5 Stonebridge Park (Willesden)–Toton coal empties on a bright sunny summer evening in 1964. These 40-ton bogie coal hoppers were designed in 1929 by the LMS to carry coal in bulk to the ex-LNWR Stonebridge Park power station, which, until its closure in 1967, provided power for the Euston–Watford DC line. Very similar wagons, but with air-operated doors, were used on the Tyne Dock–Consett iron-ore flow. The site of the power station is now occupied by the LUL Bakerloo Line depot. The train will reach the Midland main line and Toton via Northampton and Market Harborough.
Geoff Rixon

Below: Kettering-allocated No 48355 (Horwich 1944) coasts along the up slow line, approaching Bourne End (south of Berkhamsted), in a gap between a string of FA Cup Final specials on Saturday 11 May 1963 with a Class 9 block load of domestic coal for Willesden Sudbury yard. In the background (above the locomotive) is the lock-keeper's house adjacent to Bourne End top lock on the Grand Union canal. *Trevor Owen*

Right: The fireman of Willesden-allocated No 48325 (Crewe 1944) is near enough to home to decide not to bother with taking water from

Bushey troughs as they roll a long Class D express freight along the up slow line. From left to right the running lines are down and up DC lines, down and up fast lines, and down and up slow lines. The track-maintenance problems faced by the permanent-way department at water troughs, with the track regularly being soaked with spilt water, can be easily imagined in this shot from Saturday 30 April 1960. The '8F' may be grime-encrusted, but there are no visible steam leaks, the exhaust is clean and there is a 'white feather' at the safety valves, indicating a locomotive in excellent mechanical condition. *Trevor Owen*

With the shed's tall mechanical coaling plant towering in the background, Nuneaton-based No 48723 (Brighton 1944 as LNER 'O6' No 7669) is attached to the Willesden 75-ton steam breakdown crane, as they prepare to come off Willesden shed for weekend engineering work on Saturday 27 April 1963. The '7E' reporting number refers to the Weekly Ballast Circular notice item describing this pre-electrification bridge-replacement job. In the right background are several EE Type 1 'D8000' (later Class 20) diesels, of which Willesden had received an allocation of 10 by this date. The site of Willesden shed is now occupied by the EWS-operated Willesden Intermodal Terminal (formerly Willesden Freightliner Terminal). *Geoff Rixon*

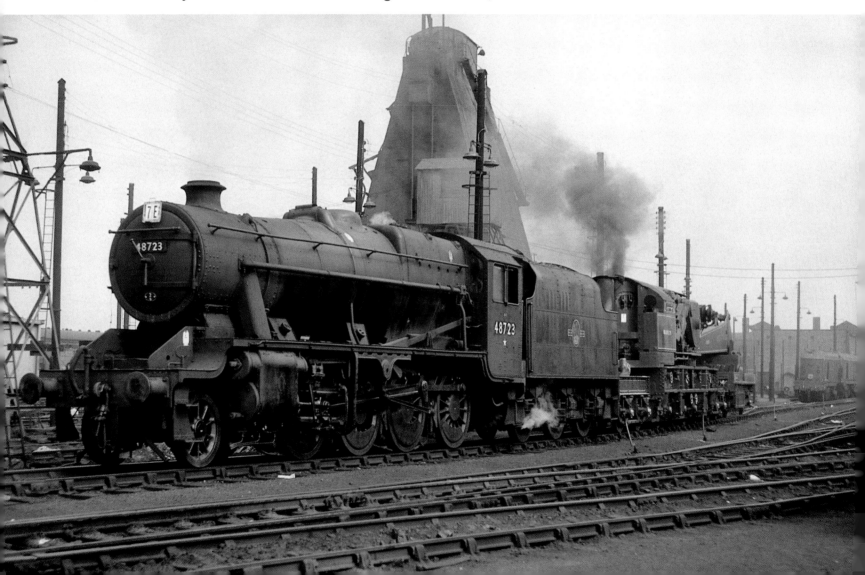

Paddington-bound commuters, featuring a sprinkling of bowler-hatted City gents, are distracted from their newspapers by Tyseley-allocated No 48415 (Swindon 1943) as she runs by with a Class H Bordesley–Acton freight on the up relief line at Twyford on Tuesday 12 May 1959. The photographer was waiting to record the passage of the 'South Wales Pullman' and 'Bristolian' expresses. Twyford is still the junction for the Henley-on-Thames branch, which curves away in the right background above the footbridge. *Trevor Owen*

WALES & THE MARCHES

Below: Shrewsbury's No 48369 (Horwich 1944) brings a Shrewsbury (Coleham)–Llandilo Junction (Llanelly) Class 5 express freight round the sharp curve on to the Central Wales line at Craven Arms on the evening of Saturday 27 July 1963. At this stage, this section retained its original double track for the 12 miles as far as Knighton. The Central Wales line was a stronghold of the '8Fs' for both freight and passenger work from 1943 to the end of through freight working in 1964. The first four and the sixth wagons on the train carry the three vertical white stripes indicating 'shock' wagons. These 'shoc vans' and 'shoc highs'/'shoc bars' had bodies mounted on shock-absorbing underframes and were designed to protect vulnerable traffics from damage during the rough-and-tumble shunting experienced in most marshalling yards. In this case the vehicles will be engaged in the carriage of tinplate from the various tinplate works in the Swansea and Llanelly areas. *Michael Mensing*

Right: Another Shrewsbury '8F' on the ex-LNWR Central Wales line, No 48724 (Brighton 1944 as LNER 'O6' No 7670) blows off impatiently as she stands at Builth Road High Level station with a Class H freight, waiting for a northbound passenger train to clear the single line from Garth, on 25 July 1959. On the right, the driver has sought refuge from his hot footplate and is looking down on to the Low Level station, perhaps observing an Ivatt '465xx' 2-6-0 arriving with a Brecon–Moat Lane connecting train. The ex-Cambrian Low Level station closed in December 1962. *Alan Jarvis*

Left: In this undated shot, taken near the top of the seven-mile climb at 1 in 82/95 from Penpergwm through Abergavenny to Llanvihangel, Shrewsbury's No 48738 (Darlington 1945 as LNER 'O6' No 3133) roars uphill with a mixed-load northbound Class 7 freight from Severn Tunnel Junction to Coton Hill. The first two wagons in the train are Conflat Ls, each loaded with three L-type containers for steel-making lime. The next three wagons are low-roofed gunpowder vans, possibly returning empty to Penrhyndeudraeth on the Cambrian Coast line after unloading commercial explosives at South Wales mines. Further down the train, behind the tank wagon, is a raft of unsheeted 'hybar' wagons, likely to be returning to Hawarden Bridge for boxed steel sheets, followed by a selection of coke hoppers, probably loaded from Cardiff to Brymbo. *Peter Alexander/Millbrook House collection*

Below: Saltley's No 48109 (Crewe 1939) gathers speed eastwards along the up relief line away from Rhymney Bridge Junction (Cardiff) towards Newport on 22 April 1963 with a Class 6 special of empty vans. On the left are Pengam sidings, until recently the site of Cardiff Freightliner Terminal. In the far distance a '56xx' leaves Pengam sidings with westbound coal empties. *Alan Jarvis*

THE WEST COUNTRY

On 22 August 1964, Burton's No 48672 (Ashford 1944) heads east at Lansdown Junction, Cheltenham, ready to cross to the up main towards Bromsgrove with an express freight. The branch on the left is the ex-GWR cross-country route to Banbury via Andoversford and Kingham. This route was shared as far as Andoversford by the Midland & South Western Junction Railway to Swindon Town and Andover. The signalbox is an LMS wartime 'ARP' design dating from the wartime remodelling which produced a triangle of lines with the new Hatherley Junction, to the west beyond Lansdown Junction. The train is a Stoke Gifford–Washwood Heath Class D with a typically mixed load, including a loaded cattle wagon, three FHGs, a 'Palbrick' specialised brick-carrying wagon, a Conflat, a vanfit, four sheeted FHGs carrying china clay and an assortment of MoD vehicles loaded on lowfits. *Tony Bowles/The Restoration & Archiving Trust*

Lyncombe Vale, between Devonshire and Combe Down tunnels, only 1¹/₂ miles from Bath Green Park, is the location for this delightful view of No 48436 (Swindon 1944) as she carefully descends the 1-in-50 grade towards Bath on 28 June 1962. The train appears to be a trip from Radstock to Bath, consisting of wagons from the Radstock wagon-repair works and locally produced domestic coal. Along term resident of St Philip's Marsh (82B), no 48436 moved to Bath Green Park for two months in 1961, but was reportedly a Shrewsbury resident by this date of this photograph. *Derek Cross*

Left: Bath Green Park-based No 48309 (Crewe 1943) proudly carries Class 1 headlamps as she leaves Combe Down Tunnel with eight malachite-green Bulleid coaches forming the repeat LCGB 'Wessex Downsman' railtour on Saturday 3 May 1965. No 48309 was a 'celebrity' '8F', having twice been involved in the haulage of Royal Trains — firstly on 26 October 1952, from Llandovery to Milford Haven, and then on 8 August 1955, jointly with No 48707, from Aberystwyth to Milford Haven. In the summer of 1952, in preparation for their royal duties, Nos 48309, 48330 and 48707 all visited Crewe Works for the fitting of carriage-warming apparatus, which was retained. Apparently Swansea Paxton Street shed found this useful afterwards, allowing it to use the locomotives on winter special passenger work over the Central Wales line, such as Rugby Union sleeping car specials to Edinburgh. No other '8Fs' are thought to have acquired this fitting before the preservation era. *Bill Gates*

Below: The much-lamented ex-Somerset & Dorset Joint Railway line from Bath to Bournemouth officially closed with effect from 7 March 1966. On the final day of regular services, Saturday 5 March 1966, No 48760 (Doncaster 1946 as LNER 'O6' No 3155) worked the morning stopping passenger train from Bath to Templecombe. Here the Bath Green Park-allocated locomotive heads this train, formed of three malachite-green Bulleid coaches, into Midford, the first station south from Bath. *Gavin Morrison*

OVERSEAS

Right-hand-drive, coal-fired and air-brake-fitted Turkish State Railways 'Churchill' TCDD No 45161 (NB 1941, WD 522) shunts at Irmak, 40 miles east of Ankara, on 30 May 1970. The guard and driver seem distracted by the herd of goats for which the noise of a steam locomotive appears to hold no terrors. The 20 Turkish 'Churchills' were replacements for a cancelled 1939 export order. WD 338-59 had been despatched in 1941, but seven were lost at sea, so WD 522-24/52/4 followed as replacements. As an export order the locomotives were sent out in a dismantled state and were re-erected in the Turkish workshops at Sivas under the direction of LMS engineer Mr R. G. Jarvis, who later in his career was responsible for the redesign and rebuilding of the Bulleid Pacifics. *Trevor Owen*

Below: Another 'Churchill', TCDD No 45167 (NB 1940, WD 352), shunting well inside Asian East Turkey at Zile, 165 miles east of Ankara, in May 1977. The absence of drop grates on these locomotives made them unsuitable for main-line work in a country where coal supplies are often of doubtful quality, so they spent most of their working lives on local trip and shunting work. *Michael Welch*

Overleaf: Right-hand-drive, oil-fired and air-braked Iraq State Railways No TD1421 (NB 1942, WD 540, ISR 41.236) is on station-pilot duty at Mosul, on the River Tigris in northern Iraq, on 21 March 1967. From here the railway leads north to Syria and Turkey. Note the auxiliary water tender attached in this arid country, where, presumably, suitable water supplies are sparse. At the end of the war 12 surplus '8Fs' (from a total of 143 '8Fs' delivered to Persia) were transferred to Iraq, travelling on metre-gauge transporter wagons as far as Baghdad. They remained at work on main-line freight and important passenger trains until the early 1970s. Some derelict long-stored examples were observed at Baghdad in 1982, and at least two are known still to have been in existence just prior to the outbreak of the Gulf War. *Basil Roberts*

Front cover: Stockport-allocated No 48626 (built Brighton 1943) storms by with a down fitted freight at Rowington troughs, south of Lapworth on the ex-GW Leamington–Birmingham main line, on the evening of 25 August 1966. *Michael Mensing*

Back cover: A Sunday morning at Royston shed (55D) in October 1966 produces an attractive line-up of eight '8Fs'. Royston shed was built by the LMS (as 20C) in 1932, complete with a housing estate for staff, and provided motive power for the busy colliery area east of Barnsley around Cudworth, including serving the collieries located on the surviving western ends of both the former Hull & Barnsley Railway and the Dearne Valley Light Railway. The shed closed to steam on 5 November 1967 but had an exclusive allocation of 24 '8Fs' as late as July 1967. The former MR main line past Royston, closed as a through route in 1986, is now the Bombardier test track for Virgin's new 'Voyager' units. *The Stanier 8F Locomotive Society collection (photographer unknown)*